THE JUSTICE GAME

A Simulation

Instructor's Manual

ALAN S. ENGEL

Miami University

with Keith DeGreen and James Rebo

GLENCOE PRESS
A division of Benziger Bruce & Glencoe, Inc.
Beverly Hills

KF
9223
.Z9
E5
Manual

147669

Copyright © 1974 by Benziger Bruce & Glencoe, Inc.

Printed in the United States of America

All rights reserved. No part of this book may be reproduced or transmitted in any form or by any means, electronic or mechanical, including photocopying, recording, or by any information storage and retrieval system, without permission in writing from the Publisher.

Glencoe Press
A division of Benziger Bruce & Glencoe, Inc.
8701 Wilshire Boulevard
Beverly Hills, California 90211

Collier-Macmillan Canada, Ltd.

First printing, 1974

Table of Contents

ABOUT THE JUSTICE GAME v

INTRODUCTION 1

1 THE GAME IN QUICK REVIEW 3

        In General 3
        Control 3
        Diagram of the Justice Game 4
        Public 5
        Suspects 5
        Police 5
        Public Attorney 5
        Private Attorney 6
        Prosecutor 6
        Court 6
        Corrections 6

2 GETTING STARTED 7

        Basic Design 7
        Time Frame 7
        Materials Required 8
        Check List for Beginning Game 8
        Instructions for "Seeded Cases" 9

3 DEBRIEFING 11

4 VARIATIONS 13

5 FINAL NOTE 14

SUPPLY OF JUSTBUCKS (SIMULATION MONEY)

About The Justice Game

New text materials are often the result of an author's dissatisfaction with the state of the art. The Justice Game is no exception. Like many of my colleagues who teach courses relating to the criminal justice system, I have long been troubled by the fact that instruction in this area tends to concentrate so heavily on the appellate process (read Supreme Court). Although understandable in many respects, this focus is also unfortunate because it deprives students of a much wider and more accurate perspective—namely, seeing the criminal justice system as a real *system,* and not merely that part of it which relates to the upper courts. In short, I felt it would be desirable to prepare materials that would teach students about the interrelationships of the criminal justice system, its workings and complexities at the grass-roots level.

Coupled with this aim was a second objective—to develop a set of materials that might really capture the interest and imagination of the student. Here again it seemed to me that the conventional approach left much to be desired. Surely, after all this time, we should be able to come up with something more inventive and stimulating than the standard text and lecture. It was that notion which led to the concept of simulation, and to the intriguing idea that we might devise a unique kind of educational experience for teaching students about the criminal justice system.

What subsequently emerged from these two operating premises was the general concept of a criminal justice simulation. The basic idea was carried forward in a graduate seminar, and improved by two of its members, Keith DeGreen and James Rebo. Ultimately it was put to the test of actual classroom use in a series of trials between 1972 and 1973. The results have been exceptionally encouraging and have prompted us to share the project with others in the discipline.

If our experience is a reliable measure, we expect others will find this simulation a highly effective learning situation, which provides students with a fresh view of the subject. Not only does it synthesize and integrate the various concepts for them; it also offers them the unique opportunity of observing the process from within. Perhaps its greatest challenge is to the instructor, who must reorient himself to the more passive role of watching from the sidelines while students learn from participation.

Introduction

Before proceeding to the mechanics of the Justice Game, it is appropriate to describe and explain the game's objectives. To understand what the simulation seeks to accomplish is to put the exercise in proper perspective. Equally important, the objectives may suggest to the instructor potential uses that would further enhance the game's educational value.

What should the Justice Game help us to teach our students? The answers which follow are based on our actual experience with it.

First, the Justice Game will *inform* students about the workings of the criminal justice system: the nature of individual components and the way those components interrelate to make an effective whole. For example, students should begin to learn about plea bargaining, arraignments, working relationships between police and prosecutor, and a variety of other basic elements of criminal justice. Some features of the simulation are purposefully designed to convey this information.

Second, the exercise is intended to communicate a sense of the system's *complexity* to students. From afar (and from in front of the television set) it is easy to see the system of criminal justice in oversimplified terms. It is not easy for the casual observer to understand that justice is the product of a highly complicated series of decisions, and that each of those decisions is itself a product of forces operating elsewhere in the system. Accordingly, the attempt to fix responsibility and to reform the process is no simple matter. Students are weaned from the tendency to seek monolithic explanations (it's all the fault of the cops) and are exposed to a more realistic view of criminal justice.

Third, the simulation is intended to provide insight into the effect of *extralegal variables* on the outcome of the legal process. Students quickly perceive that what passes for justice is a product not merely of laws and the official institutional apparatus, but also of personalities, political pressures, the sociology of the system itself, and chance. Each part of the system is influenced by its counterparts, and each part is ultimately influenced by the feedback consequences of its own behavior.

Fourth, as a corollary of all this, the student cannot fail to recognize that no part of the criminal justice system is without strain, conflict, *cross-pressures,* and a rather generous share of frustration. Hence, a conviction-minded public wants its prosecutor to run up a good batting average in court (and thereby reduce the costs of crime to society). So, too, the police, who have already invested time and energy in preparing the case. But a prosecutor who will not make deals—or who attempts to pursue all cases with the same intensity, without attaching differential priorities—is likely to confront a new set of pressures from the court and corrections. Moreover, he is likely to fail in his mission. And that, of course, is the lesson common to all parts of the system, from which none can escape.

Our fifth objective speaks to the problem of sensitizing the student to the very real dangers of *alienation* within the system. While some students are already painfully aware of that condition, others have yet to perceive just what the condition is or how alienation occurs. Still others need to gain an understanding of how the roles themselves can defeat even the most dedicated efforts to render justice in a less automated and less depersonalized setting.

Sixth, another important teaching concerns the impact of *time and delay* on the outcome of criminal justice. What the simulation seeks to accomplish in this respect is an awareness of how the clock affects the variety of interests involved. Students need to learn, for example, how delay may benefit the case of the defendant, as well as how it can injure him in the loss of liberty while awaiting trial.

A seventh aim goes directly to the point of *ideal versus reality*. Here the objective is to bring students to a clearer understanding of the disparity between the civics book model of criminal justice and the practical realities. Among other things, students are obliged to confront the problem of the differential treatment accorded citizens of different backgrounds before the law. Further, the simulation requires them to seriously weigh the necessity for bargaining and compromise against the idealized concept of pure justice.

Eighth, the Justice Game is intended to sharply emphasize that every decision carries with it a cost consequence. For the student who assumes the role of the police officer, the choice is whether to give equal attention to all crimes (cost equals impossibility), or to give priority to victimless crimes (cost equals inattention to more serious lawbreaking), or to give priority to felonies (cost equals a reduced volume of arrests). Each participant in the simulation is presented with a cost-benefit choice of this sort, and each student is forced to the realization that no decision is cost-free.

Our ninth objective can best be described as an intentional effort to force the student into a serious reexamination of his previous attitudes toward the system of criminal justice. For those who approach the subject with the conviction that the system is totally devoid of reason, and who are contemptuous of its workings, the aim is to substitute understanding for condemnation. Conversely, where the predisposition is toward a complacent acceptance of the system, the aim is to unsettle the student and place him in a more critical frame of mind. In sum, the end goal is that our participants may come to see the criminal justice system as a functioning mixture of both strengths and weaknesses.

Finally, one more purpose bears mention. Though the primary function of the Justice Game is instructional, and while it was explicitly designed to serve as an educational device, its potential extends beyond the classroom. Since a simulation can serve as a human laboratory, it offers the social scientist some choice possibilities for experimental study. Thus, the Justice Game may well provide an important research facility for the testing of various propositions about the law and the mechanisms for its enforcement. By the same token, it can provide students with an exploratory area from which new hypotheses may be identified.

The preceding list only touches on a few possible uses this exercise may serve. It has been our finding that the value of the experience broadens as the simulation progresses, and further insights may be achieved by student and instructor alike.

1 The Game in Quick Review

IN GENERAL

The first thing you will need to know about the actual operation of the simulation is how it is organized. That information is detailed in the *Student's Manual*. Here it will be briefly summarized to provide the instructor with an overview and a convenient reference guide.

In general, the Justice Game is a point-to-point simulation, with players entering the exercise in relation to the occurrence of a crime, and exiting at the disposition of that case. The simulation is sustained by two built-in mechanisms: one, there is an abundant supply of cases to keep the game going for a considerable period of time (several hours, after which they can be repeated); two, the disposition of each case automatically incurs a number of feedback consequences which are likely to influence various parts of the simulation. Thus, provision has been made to keep it continuous and changing.

The most convenient way to relate to the structure, roles, and operation of the Justice Game is to refer to the diagram that follows (for Diagram 1, see student manual). There are nine agencies or institutions with which the simulation deals: Control, Police, Public, Court, Suspects, Public Defender, Private Attorney, Prosecutor, and Corrections. The number of students assigned to play these roles varies (we'll talk about that in the next section), but there's room for every student to participate in the simulation.

The nine component roles are designed to represent the major institutional aspects of our criminal justice system. In addition to the roles which portray the various governmental interests, there is also a representation of key sectors of the public, and the persons who stand accused of crime. In short, the simulation attempts to create a kind of miniaturized society.

In this scaled-down version of society, crimes will occur with some frequency, and each participant—public, suspect, official—must decide on a course of action with respect to those cases. A variety of outcomes are possible in every instance (victims may or may not be willing to press the complaint, witnesses may or may not cooperate, police have discretion to arrest and charge, defendants may or may not be willing to bargain for a lighter sentence, etc.). While playing the game students get to see the system from the perspective of public, defendant, or establishment. Ultimately, they also get to see the consequences of their decisions. As cases are won or lost, the cost to the public will be affected, and so too will be the fortunes of the public officials—who retain or lose office depending upon the success or failure of their decisions.

To better understand how the typical case proceeds, and how each role functions, the nine major component roles are briefly summarized.

CONTROL

The primary function of Control is to keep the simulation operating. To do this, two responsibilities have to be met: crimes have to be fed into the system at proper intervals, and taxes have to be collected from the public in accordance with the outcome of each case. The first responsibility is assigned to a crime initiator, who introduces a new crime every two minutes. (Note: the simulation is "seeded" with nine crimes already in progress at the opening session—the purpose being to involve most participants from the very beginning.) The crime initiator draws new crimes from a list provided in the student manual appendix, alternating between those with a victim and those without (even and odd numbers, respectively). To issue a crime, the initiator writes its number on the top of Form A (Criminal Case Record) and takes it either to the public (crimes with victims) or to the police (victimless crimes). Every crime has a twenty-minute expiration time, to prevent stalling and help keep the pressure on. To keep track, the crime initiator uses Form B (Tally Sheet).

The tax collector sees to the other main responsibility of Control, assessing the public at the conclusion of each case. He does this by using

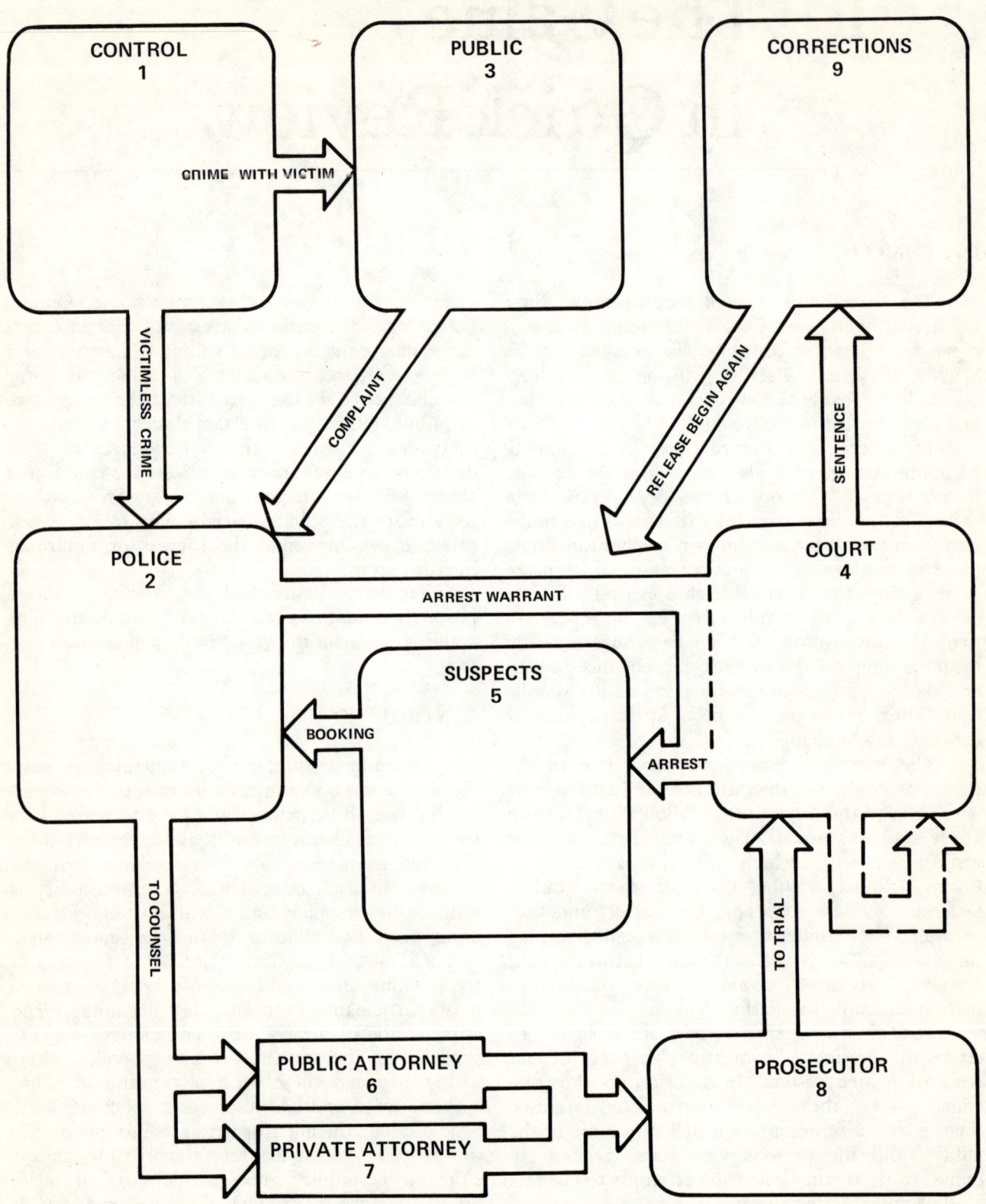

DIAGRAM 2: THE JUSTICE GAME

Beginning with Control (1) crimes are introduced to Police (2) or Public (3). In latter case Police must have complaint to proceed. Arrest requires Warrant from Court (4). Then Suspect is arrested (5) and booked at station (2). Suspect then confers with Public Attorney (6) or Private Attorney (7), and with attorney proceeds to Prosecutor (8) and then to Court (4) for two appearances. Non-prison cases return to Suspect Pool (5) while persons under sentence proceed to Corrections (9) and then to Suspect Pool upon release. Case record is returned to Control (1) for assessment of taxes and then to Taxpayer-Validator in the Public (3), whenever the case has been resolved.

the cost chart (student manual, page 11) to calculate the cost to various members of the public (victim, witness, taxpayer). The cost is based on three factors: the extent of public cooperation, whether or not an arrest was made, and whether the case was won or lost. The tax collector can determine that cost by examining the criminal case record, which is turned in whenever a case finishes out. Payment is in "Justbucks," a simulation currency provided to the members of the public ($1500 each). You will find this currency, which you are to distribute to the public at the beginning of the game, in the back of this manual.

An optional role which can also be assigned to Control is that of reporter, to help publicize the performance of various other participants.

PUBLIC

The public is a symbolic representation of the larger society. Its primary function is to reflect three crucial interests: victim, witness, and taxpayer. In the interests of economy, the same persons continue to play the same roles for each case. As cases are brought to them by the crime initiator, victim and witness must decide whether to press the complaint forward. Their decisions will be predicated in part on the cost chart previously referred to (student manual, page 11). They must balance the possible cost of involving themselves against the possible cost of failing to get involved. The taxpayer is not involved in the decisions of victim and witness, but must nonetheless bear the consequences of their choices when the collector comes around.

An important responsibility, one that befits his observer status, is assigned to the taxpayer: he must evaluate the performance of the various other role players in the game. In this role, defined as taxpayer-validator, he tallies the wins and losses on Form F (Score Sheet). The crucial performance level requirements are as follows:

- Police must make an arrest in 80 percent of all cases.
- Private attorney must win acquittals in at least 50 percent of his cases.
- Public Defender must win acquittals in at least 50 percent of all nonplea-bargained cases.
- Prosecutor must win convictions in at least 50 percent of all nonplea-bargained cases.
- Judge must not allow more than 25 percent of cases to expire before verdict.

Failure to meet these quotas means the officeholder may lose his position. At the end of each hour, the instructor should replace those role players who have not met their assigned quotas.

SUSPECTS

All persons without an official or public role are assigned to the suspect pool, and become defendants to accompany the crime records. This helps to personalize the criminal justice experience both for those who deal with and those who play defendants. To make the simulation still more real, suspects are identified as either "A" or "B" class citizens, and their treatment (in terms of accessibility to private versus public attorney, and the availability of bail) differs accordingly. When the police have decided to make an arrest, and have secured the necessary court order, they may arbitrarily attach any suspect to the crime record, and that defendant then proceeds to go through the system, playing out the necessary role. "Used" suspects simply return to the pool to await their next assignment (unless they are convicted and sent to corrections).

POLICE

The police confront two types of crime about which they must make decisions. Victimless crimes are brought directly to their attention by the crime initiator, while the public notifies them of crimes with victims. In either case, an arrest requires these actions on their part: a decision to make the arrest, the procurement of an arrest order from the court, the procurement of a suspect (to whom the Miranda Warning must be read), and the provision of an attorney (the kind depends on the class of citizen involved). Police have the usual discretion to arrest or not, and a choice in determining the degree of guilt if an arrest is made. Their other obligations include appearing in court at the time of trial, and escorting prisoners under sentence to corrections. As previously noted, they have an 80 percent arrest quota to meet. The role is structured as to make this difficult to accomplish unless they conserve their resources carefully.

PUBLIC ATTORNEY

Persons arrested are entitled to counsel, but the less fortunate citizens (class "B") do not enjoy the luxury of a private attorney, and must instead depend upon the public defender. Because the public defender handles more cases than the private attorney, he is less likely to have time for his clients; consequently, the "B" citizen's disadvantage is reinforced. The public attorney needs a 50 percent acquittal rate (in nonplea-bargained cases) to stay in office.

PRIVATE ATTORNEY

Preferred citizens ("A" class) are given the possible benefit of a private attorney. Except that he will undoubtedly handle fewer cases, his responsibilities and role are the same as the public attorney. As to quota, there is one difference: whereas the public attorney must win acquittals in 50 percent of all nonplea-bargained cases, the private attorney must win acquittals in 50 percent of all his cases—a higher standard of performance.

PROSECUTOR

After a suspect has conferred with his attorney, the prosecutor enters the case and decides with what crime to charge the suspect. That decision may be made independently, in conjunction with the police, or in negotiation with the defendant and his attorney. The prosecutor has considerable discretion in the matter, as do the police, and he may decide to drop the case or pursue it vigorously. Ultimately, it is he who will take it to court. In at least 50 percent of his nonplea-bargained cases, he must win convictions to keep office.

COURT

Prosecuted cases appear twice in court. The first hearing represents a composite of several appearances that would take place in the real world. It is intended to represent—combined into one—the initial appearance, preliminary hearing, indictment, and arraignment. (For the sake of authenticity, as well as for its educational value, the judge is obliged to read the defendant a statement explaining this representation.) At the conclusion of this first stage, the defendant (through his attorney) enters a plea and exercises his option to choose the type of trial. The case is then set down for trial (with the class "A" citizens free to wait in the comfort of the suspect pool, while "B" citizens must stand in line). At the second appearance—the actual trial—the court has before it a suspect, police officer, defense attorney, and prosecutor, and is presided over by a judge. The judge hears the case (both sides may improvise the oral argument as they wish, given the scenario of the criminal incident report). In a bench trial, the judge renders a decision based on his assessment of the testimony. To simulate jury trials (without the encumbrance of an involved procedure and large numbers of students) we employ a probability table (see student manual, pages 23 and 41). The judge covers various numbered squares in the table, more and more as the odds increase against the defendant—for example, as both victim and witness agree to testify. Ultimately, the defendant is asked to pick a number between one and ten, and if he selects one of the squares that are still uncovered, he is considered innocent. If acquitted, the defendant returns to the suspect pool; but if convicted it is up to the judge to determine his sentence. Sentences are calculated in minutes of confinement at the corrections institution. The judge, as previously noted, must rule on 75 percent of all cases, excluding those previously terminated for reasons other than expiration of time.

CORRECTIONS

Where a time sentence has been imposed by the judge, and is to be served, a commitment order directs that the defendant be taken by police to the warden. To simulate the grim realities, we urge that the prison have a limited capacity (two chairs) and that punishment take the form of a purposeless, irritating, and degrading activity. (Students are uncommonly imaginative at inventing these.) Examples include copying law review articles backwards, or sitting with a paper bag over the head (solitary confinement). Upon release, the player is returned to the suspect pool to await further assignment in the form of a new arrest.

It is at this point, or whenever the case may have terminated, that the criminal record is returned to Control for the computation of taxes, taxes are collected, and the taxpayer-validator takes note of the various wins and losses.

2 Getting Started

BASIC DESIGN

We turn now to the nuts and bolts of putting the simulation into the classroom. How exactly does one go about it?

The first requirement is a sufficient number of students. We suggest twenty as the minimum required to fill the defined roles and allow for suspects:

Control (Initiator & Tax Collector)	2
Public (Victim, Witness, Taxpayer)	3
Police	2
Attorneys (Public, Private)	2
Prosecutor	1
Judge	1
Warden	1
Suspects	8
TOTAL	20

The eight suspects are needed to provide for several cases in progress when the simulation commences, with additional suspects available as the need arises.

As the class size increases from twenty, the added numbers may be involved in a variety of different ways. The student manual defines an optional reporter's role for the Control group. Others can be used in the suspect pool. At a total of thirty players, you might seriously consider the addition of one extra police officer and another judge. Those two roles tend to bear the heaviest pressures in the simulation. For classes which number forty or more students, there are several options. One is simply to increase the number of players in each role, or alternatively to split the group into two sections of twenty each. There is also a variation of the Justice Game, on a much larger scale, which we have experimented with quite successfully; it is described on page 13.

Regarding the level of student for which the game is appropriate, we know from experience that it has succeeded not only with all levels of college and university students, but also with high school seniors and non-college adults. The preparation time required has been minimal for all those we have worked with, which suggests to us that the roles are very easily assimilated.

One final comment on the subject of the players: the simulation seems equally feasible regardless of whether students volunteer for their roles or the instructor assigns them. On balance, we tend to prefer the latter arrangement, because it enables one to capitalize on certain personality types by placing them in certain roles. For example, a good candidate for judge is the conscientious student who is a stickler for details. Equally interesting is the selection of an idealistic student to serve as police officer.

TIME FRAME

On the subject of time it might be useful to differentiate between minimum requirements and optimum use.

As noted, participants can rapidly acquaint themselves with their roles. Since a player is obliged to read only the introductory section of the manual and that portion which relates to his own role, even the most complicated assignment can be grasped within an hour. As to the actual simulation run, anywhere from forty-five to sixty minutes works very well. Finally, one can cover a substantial amount of ground in another hour's discussion. All told, therefore, a period of three hours—or even just two in class, with the other one as overnight reading—is all that is required to put the simulation into operation.

Where time permits, however, a series of five one-hour sessions would be an ideal arrangement. Assuming the manual reading is assigned for outside of class, the first three sessions could be used for the simulation exercise, followed by two hourly discussion sessions. The three hours of simulation are suggested because it can be extremely useful to have students engage in some role exchange at the second or third runs. For example, there is considerable educational value in moving a witness to the victim's position, or putting a police officer in the defense attorney's role, or switching between prosecutor and suspect. Two hourly discussions are urged because the simulation raises a host of issues and questions participants will want to comment on, and a single hour is not really enough time to explore these problems in depth.

When to schedule the simulation depends, of course, on the class schedule and the objectives of the instructor. While it is useful to introduce the game after case readings on due process have been completed, it could serve equally well as a motivational device at the very beginning of the course.

MATERIALS REQUIRED

Beyond having enough people and enough time, there are a few added suggestions which should help to secure the best results from the Justice Game. No special facilities are required—the conventional classroom seems to suffice quite nicely, with slight rearrangement of the furniture. The general plan is to position the various role stations around the periphery of the room (Control in one corner, followed by public along one wall, police in the next corner, attorneys along the wall, prosecutor at the next corner, then court and corrections) and use the center for the suspect pool. If there is one large single desk (i.e., the instructor's), it is best given to the court. The other agencies can operate fairly well with student arm-chair desks. Of course, a room with multiple tables would be even better. Whatever the case, it is useful to identify each agency station with an appropriate sign.

Over and above the physical facilities, the following items usually come in handy: a supply of convention-style ID tags; a felt-tip marker to identify each participant in the room; poker chips or something similar for the judge to use to cover the squares on the probability table; a gavel for the judge; and an "instrument of punishment" for the warden (the duller the book, the better).

CHECK LIST FOR BEGINNING GAME

For the sake of a smooth-running game, we recommend that the instructor follow the steps below to prepare the simulation exercise.

Pre-simulation

1. Assign roles and readings (part one of student manual plus section pertaining to role assigned) to each student. Remind students to bring manuals with them to the simulation.
2. Collect from students all the forms supplied in the back of the students' manuals.
3. Assemble the Justbucks (simulation money), which have been provided at the back of this manual. Divide into allotments of $1500 each for victim, witness, and taxpayer.
4. Prepare nine criminal case records (Form A) for distribution at the beginning of the simulation. Instructions on how to fill out those nine case records appear on pages 9-10. Remember to record the crime number and expiration time for each case on Form B (Tally Sheet), which will be given to the Control crime initiator.
5. Prepare ID tags for all players, designating roles. Remember that suspect tags should designate half the citizens as class "A" and half as class "B."
6. Prepare signs to identify each station in the simulation (i.e., Control, Public, Police Headquarters, Suspect Pool, Defense Attorneys, Prosecutor, Court, and Corrections).

Simulation

1. Prepare room by arranging furniture and attaching signs to station locations.
2. Distribute ID tags to students.
3. Direct students to proper station locations.
4. Distribute Justbucks to members of public, and distribute various forms to appropriate stations (Forms A and B to Control, Forms C, D, and E to the court, Form F to the taxpayer-validator in the public). Be sure the crime initiator understands the partially completed Form B which is given to him. (See item 4 above.) Also distribute gavel and chips to court, and punishment book to warden.
5. At this point you might wish to run a sample case through the system, commenting at each point on the procedures that people in each role are supposed to follow. Check to ensure that all players understand the responsibilities involved in their roles and answer any questions they may have. Keep discussion brief, and urge students to consult their manuals for explanation of all procedural details.
6. Introduce the nine prepared cases into the simulation. Criminal case records for crimes 1 through 4 should be given to the court. (Assign an "A" suspect to crimes 1 and 2, and "B" suspects to crimes 3 and 4. The persons named as suspects should accompany the case to court.) The case record for crime 5 (with the suspect named on it) should be taken to police headquarters. Issue crimes 6 and 8 to the victim in the public, and tell the

crime initiator to collect 200 Justbucks from the victim for those crimes. Issue crimes 7 and 9 to the police.

7. Instruct students to begin carrying out their assigned responsibilities.

INSTRUCTIONS FOR "SEEDED CASES" AT BEGINNING OF SIMULATION

The following directions will assist the instructor in preparing the nine criminal case records which are used to begin the simulation. These nine cases are "in progress" when the simulation opens. Since the cases have progressed to different stages in the simulation, each record must be filled out differently, as indicated below.

Criminal Case Record for Incident 1

    Criminal Incident Number: 1
    Expiration Time: 5 minutes after game commences
    Victim section: leave blank since crime is victimless
    Witness section: ditto
    Suspect: any "A" citizen you choose
    Citizen designation: "A"
    Arresting Officer: name of either police officer
    Offense charged: Alcoholism
    Legal Code Number: 101
    Degree: first
    Defense Attorney: name of person assigned to role of public attorney
    Confession line: blank
    Prosecutor: name of person playing that role
    Offense charged: Alcoholism
    Legal Code Number: 101
    Degree: second
    Defendant's plea: check Not Guilty
    Trial requested: check Judge
    Remainder: blank

Criminal Case Record for Incident 2

    Criminal Incident Number: 2
    Expiration time: 7 minutes into the simulation
    Victim: name of person assigned to that role
    Amount lost: 50 Justbucks
    Complaint: check Yes, victim willing to sign
    Witness: use name of person assigned that role
    Witness cooperation: check No
    Suspect: name of any with "A" designation
    Citizen designation: "A"
    Arresting Officer: name of other police officer
    Offense charged: Grand Larceny
    Legal Code Number: 111
    Degree: second
    Defense attorney: name of private attorney
    Confession line: blank
    Prosecutor: same as Incident 1
    Offense charged: Grand Larceny
    Legal Code Number: 111
    Degree: second
    Defendant's Plea: check Not Guilty
    Remainder: blank

Criminal Case Record for Incident 3

    Criminal Incident Number: 3
    Expiration time: 9 minutes into simulation
    Victim section: blank
    Witness section: blank
    Suspect: any "B" citizen from suspect pool
    Citizen designation: "B"
    Arresting Officer: same as Incident 1
    Offense charged: Alcoholism
    Legal Code Number: 101
    Degree: first
    Defense Attorney: name of public attorney
    Confession line: blank
    Prosecutor: same as Incident 1
    Remainder: blank

Criminal Case Record for Incident 4

    Criminal Incident Number: 4
    Expiration time: 11 minutes into simulation
    Victim: same as Incident 2
    Amount lost: 100 Justbucks
    Complaint: check Yes
    Witness section: same as Incident 2
    Suspect: any "B" citizen from suspect pool
    Citizen designation: "B"
    Arresting officer: same as Incident 2
    Offense charged: Grand Larceny
    Legal Code Number: 111
    Degree: second
    Defense attorney: name of public attorney
    Confession line: blank
    Prosecutor: same as Incident 1
    Remainder: blank

Criminal Case Record for Incident 5

    Criminal Incident Number: 5
    Expiration time: 13 minutes into simulation
    Victim section: blank
    Witness section: blank

Suspect: any "B" citizen
Citizen designation: "B"
Arresting Officer: either one
Remainder: blank

Criminal Case Record for Incident 6

Criminal Incident Number: 6
Expiration time: 15 minutes into simulation
Victim: same as Incident 2
Amount lost: 50 Justbucks
Complaint: blank
Witness: same as Incident 2
Witness cooperation: blank
Remainder: blank

Criminal Case Record for Incident 7

Criminal Incident Number: 7
Expiration time: 17 minutes into simulation
Remainder: blank

Criminal Case Record for Incident 8

Criminal Incident Number: 8
Expiration time: 19 minutes into simulation
Victim: same as Incident 2
Amount lost: 150 Justbucks
Witness: same as Incident 2
Witness cooperation: blank
Remainder: blank

Criminal Case Record for Incident 9

Criminal Incident Number: 9
Expiration time: 20 minutes into simulation
Remainder: blank

3 Debriefing

Since the post-simulation discussion is of the utmost importance, it is deserving of some special comment here. Past experience with the Justice Game suggests that no prodding is needed to get the students going. If anything, the problem is quite different—motivation runs so high that it is difficult to contain and channel the discussion into an orderly exchange. Techniques for systematizing the discussion will vary, but one suggestion is to proceed first to the various roles, asking each player in order for his reactions, and then move to the more general questions. Usually, as the discussion progresses around the room, from victim to witness to taxpayer to police and so on, the comments will approach a number of the areas the instructor would like to analyze. In any event, the list of annotated questions that follows may be helpful (though it by no means exhausts the potential points of interest and concern).

1. What did you learn? The question is not so naive as it sounds. Students often profit from being confronted directly by a question that forces them to reexamine the entire experience. Along the same lines: What shocked or most surprised you about the experience?

2. How accurate was the simulation? Or the corollary: In what respects was the simulation unreal? This is a more complex question because it presumes that the students have a fairly accurate perception of criminal justice procedures in the real world. That, in turn, depends upon the extent of students' previous acquaintance with the field. Where they have read extensively beforehand, it will be easy to judge whether or not they have assimilated those readings. Where they have approached the simulation "cold," their answers will enable the instructor to define those areas where misinformation and confusion are greatest. This question might also be worded: What could be done to make the simulation more realistic or authentic?

3. A useful way of directing discussion toward a number of the objectives identified at the beginning of this manual is to ask students whether they felt the system rendered justice, and if not, why not? If justice is imperfect under the system, where does the fault lie? What usually surfaces here is a biting attack (especially from victim, taxpayer, and suspects), which quickly reaches to the problems of alienation, system complexity, cross-pressures, the influence of extralegal variables and the basic conflict between idealists and pragmatists. To follow this up, ask what reforms students would suggest to improve the system, and what difficulties they see in obtaining those improvements.

4. A related issue concerns the difficulties which students perceive in the playing of various roles. Here the question is: What does the public fail to understand about the problems confronting your role? This line of questioning is intended to reveal the other side of the coin—to generate a defense of the system from those operating within it. In many instances, those who played "Establishment" roles will understand the situation very differently than does the outside public.

5. If the considerations of time and delay have not surfaced during the earlier comments from each role player, it may be useful to tackle the issue head-on with the question: In what ways does time affect the outcome of criminal justice? It is fairly predictable that the lawyers, the suspects, and the judge will have some strong views on the subject.

6. A particularly interesting discussion can be generated about the logic of the cost-benefit table which is used throughout by taxpayer, victim, witness, and tax collector. Students should be asked about the validity of this table in terms of its underlying assumptions. Can they identify the premises, and would they agree with them? The rationale behind the table, of course, is that—to varying degrees—victims, witnesses, and taxpayers all have something to lose when crimes are committed. The cost to each is obviously a product of three considerations: the cooperation factor, the arrest factor, and the outcome of the case. To symbolize this cost, the table assumes the following: that a victim usually fails to recover his entire loss; that personal involvement of victim or witness in cooperating with the authorities incurs

some cost (10 Justbucks); that use of the governmental apparatus involves some cost (10 Justbucks per prosecution); and that failure to apprehend the culprit in a crime would also inflict a cost (20 Justbucks per criminal-at-large). Consequently, it is possible for a victim to incur a maximum cost of 100 percent of whatever he lost from the crime plus 40 Justbucks to boot. That occurs where the victim agrees to cooperate, an arrest follows, and the case is lost. Conversely, if a criminal is captured and convicted, but without the victim cooperating, the victim's cost would be only 20 percent of the original loss plus 10 Justbucks.

7. The matter of jury trials, and their simulation by probability table, is another area ripe for discussion. There is usually a very heated exchange if the instructor asks: Is it reasonable to attempt to reduce a jury trial to a probability calculation? Why or why not? Equally interesting is the issue of the factors which have been considered in working out the probability: presence or absence of prosecutor, existence of a confession from the defendant, cooperation of the victim and witness, evidence of a proper arrest warrant, and presence or absence of the defense attorney and arresting officer. A related question concerns the differential weights which have been attached to each of these considerations.

8. At some point it would be interesting to get into the questions of bias and discrimination; one aspect of this issue is built into the simulation in the form of a two-class citizenry. Students should confront this problem, along with other possible evidences of inequalities in the application of criminal justice.

9. The influence of victimless crimes is an important element in the game, deserving some explicit discussion with the students. In particular, it may be useful to probe the extent to which people in various roles were conscious of differentiated types of crime, and how they reacted to each.

10. Finally, it is important to bring up the matter of feedback, and to explore the perceptions of the students on this subject. To what extent do they recognize the continuing influence of their decisions on the other aspects of the system, and on themselves?

4 Variations

One of the fascinating aspects about a simulation is its potential for adaptation and experiment, and the Justice Game is no exception. There are an endless number of embellishments, refinements, and options which can be worked into the basic design. To illustrate, and to encourage thinking about additional possibilities for experimentation, a few intriguing ideas are included here.

1. Roles may be added, as suggested earlier, in the form of a reporter, extra police, or alternating judge. It would also be possible to institute a new role factor—such as a mayor—to create still more pressures and interrelationships.

2. Rules may be modified or added, such as variations in case time expirations, Justbuck allowances, or quota requirements to stay in office. One interesting experiment along these lines would be the introduction of a new opportunity for the public to "purchase" an additional police officer by paying a high premium in Justbucks, or by an increase in taxes. Another would be to require that the police obtain confessions in 20 percent of all cases for which they make arrests.

3. The game may be expanded in its overall dimensions by the addition of some complementary feature, such as an appellate process or a human jury system.

4. If the class involves 40 or more students it becomes possible to introduce a larger public in lieu of the symbolic three-person public in the basic game. To do this, a few modifications are required. First, the entire group is to be regarded as taxpayers (the validator function is relocated in Control). Second, no Justbucks are distributed to taxpayers, as the size of the public makes collection an unwieldy task. Instead, each student is instructed to bookkeep his finances on a sheet of paper, starting with $1500 at the top and deducting various amounts as directed by the Validator after the resolution of each case. Into the midst of this public, Control introduces its crimes by arbitrarily selecting a taxpayer to be a victim and another to be a witness. The game proceeds from there as usual—the victim must decide whether to file a complaint with the police, and the witness must decide whether to cooperate. In this case, however, they are obliged to actually go to the police station. With enough people to represent the taxpaying public, it is even possible to go a step further and have the victim and witness appear at trial.

These examples only scratch the surface of the possible variations. Adaptation and experimentation are encouraged, with one caveat: bear in mind that there is a constant temptation to introduce more and more complications to the game (often for the legitimate purpose of increasing authenticity) and that each new complexity increases the danger of obscuring the basic mission of the simulation in a maze of rules and roles.

5 Final Note

For those who are old hands at the game of simulation, this parting word may be superfluous; but it may be helpful for those who are new to the experience. As with most simulations, the Justice Game is likely to produce two very striking effects. First, the usual calm of the classroom gives way to a good deal of apparent disorder and confusion—until one discovers that behind the disarray is a rather substantial amount of student learning and intense motivation. It is a very different—and much more exciting—experience than standing behind the lectern, watching all the pencils go. The second consequence (which takes some getting used to) is that students appear to be far less dependent on the instructor, with the latter relegated to a sidelines role while the class proceeds, rather effectively, to teach itself. But that reversal should not be mistaken for instructorless instruction. There is still substantial need for guidance and direction in the learning process. The teacher is a vital part of the simulation experience.

6 Supply of Justbucks (simulation money)

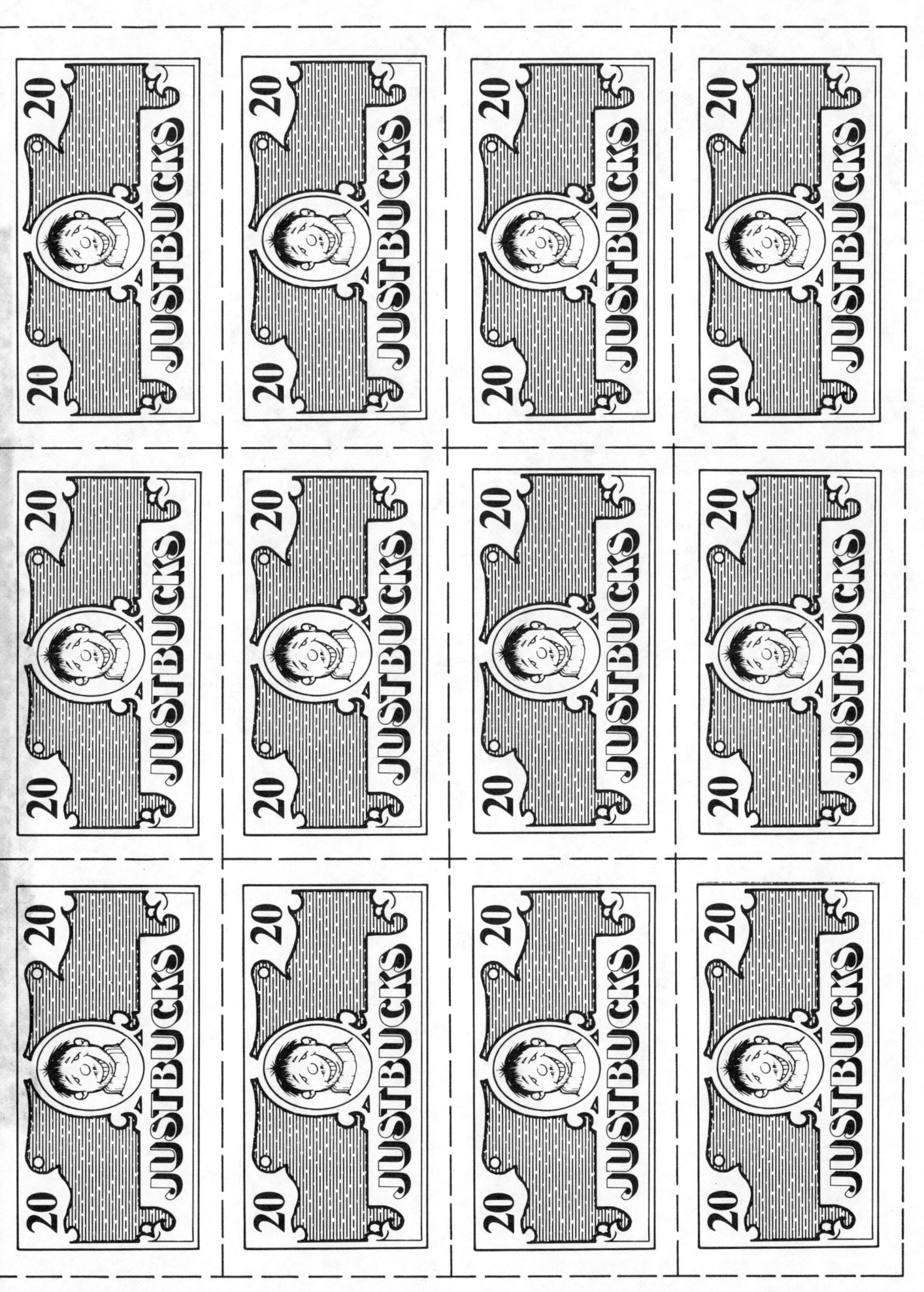

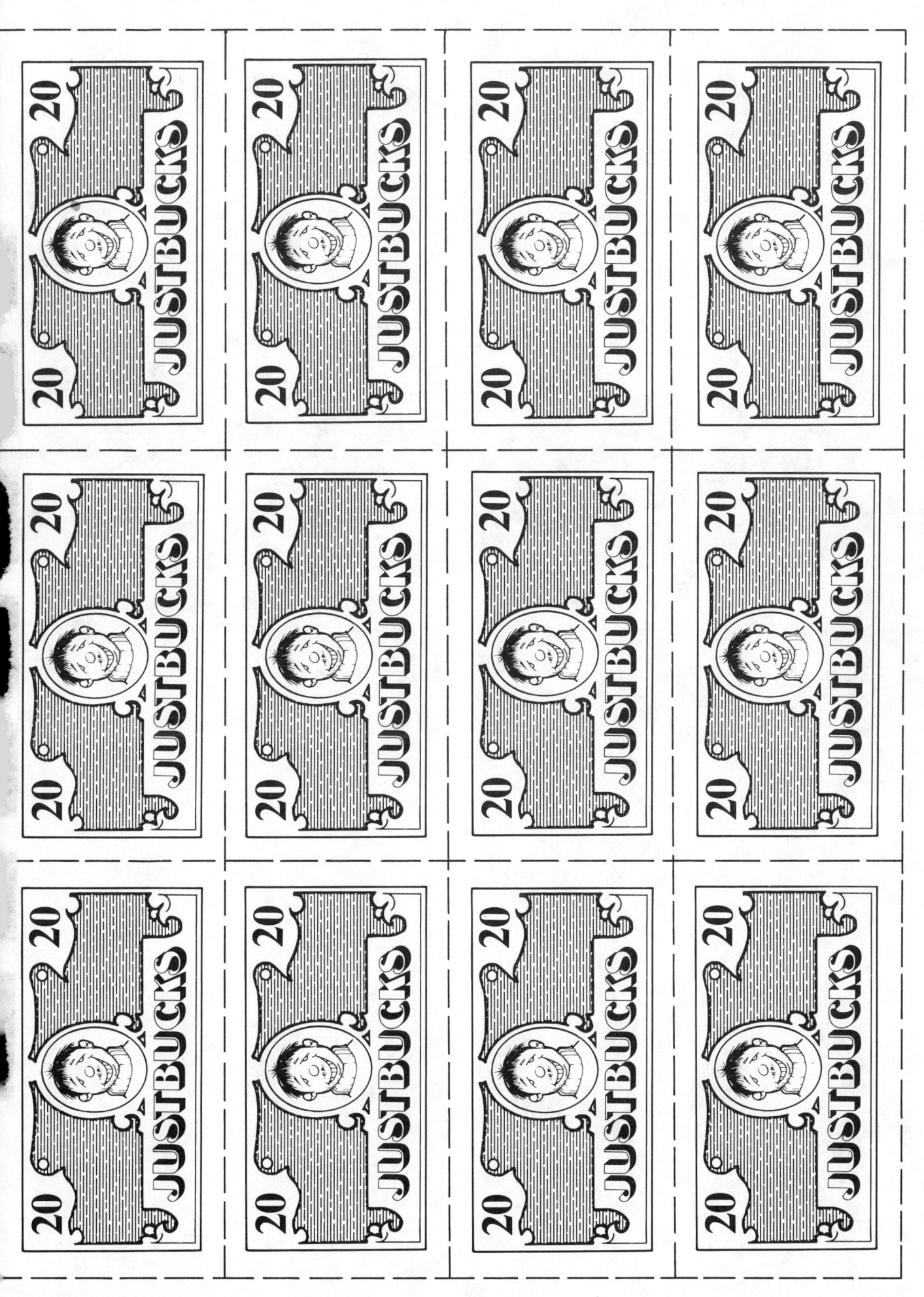

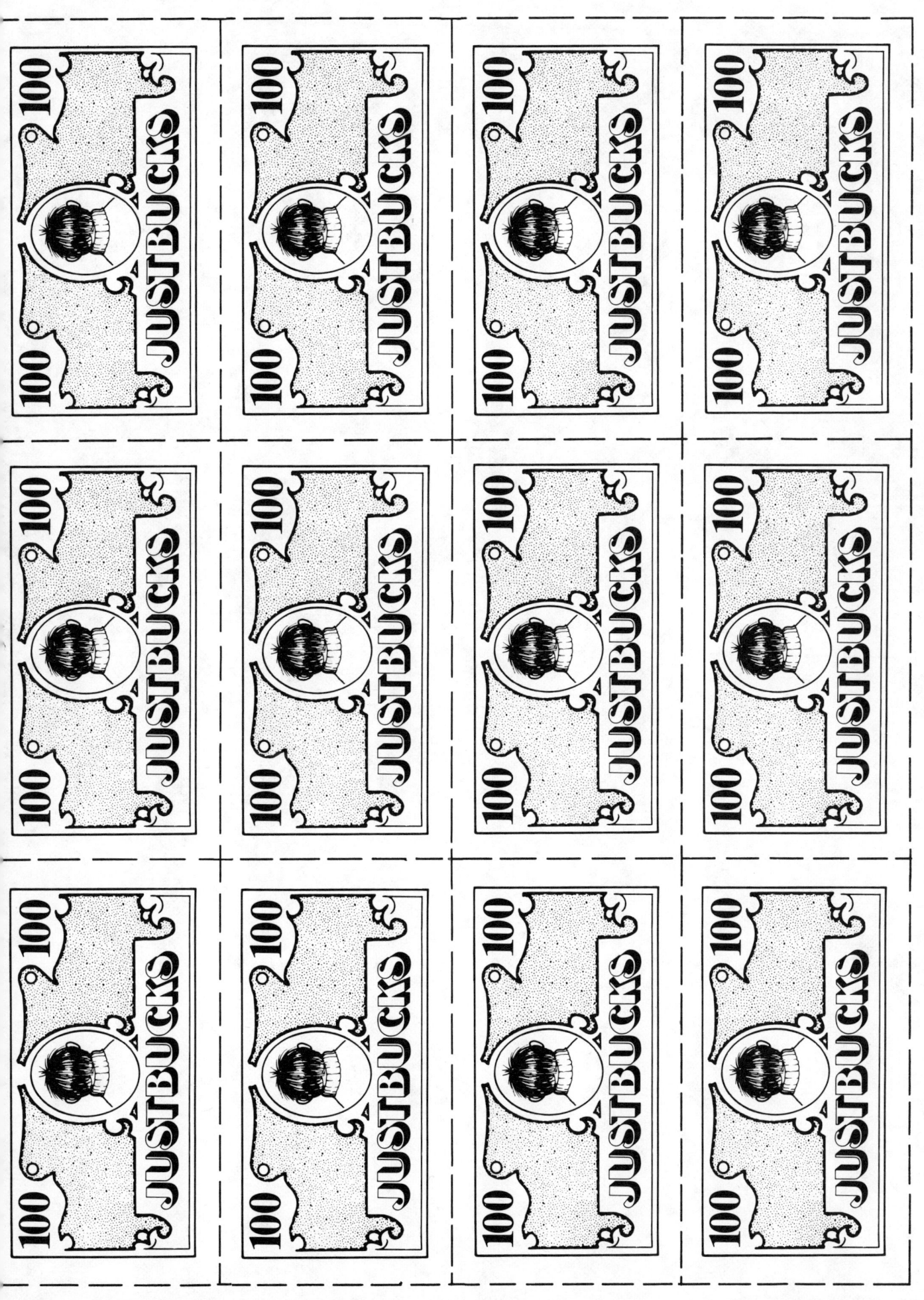

100
100
JUSTBUCKS

100
100
JUSTBUCKS

100
100
JUSTBUCKS

100
100
JUSTBUCKS

100
100
JUSTBUCKS

100
100
JUSTBUCKS

100
100
JUSTBUCKS

100
100
JUSTBUCKS

100
100
JUSTBUCKS

100
100
JUSTBUCKS

100
100
JUSTBUCKS

100
100
JUSTBUCKS

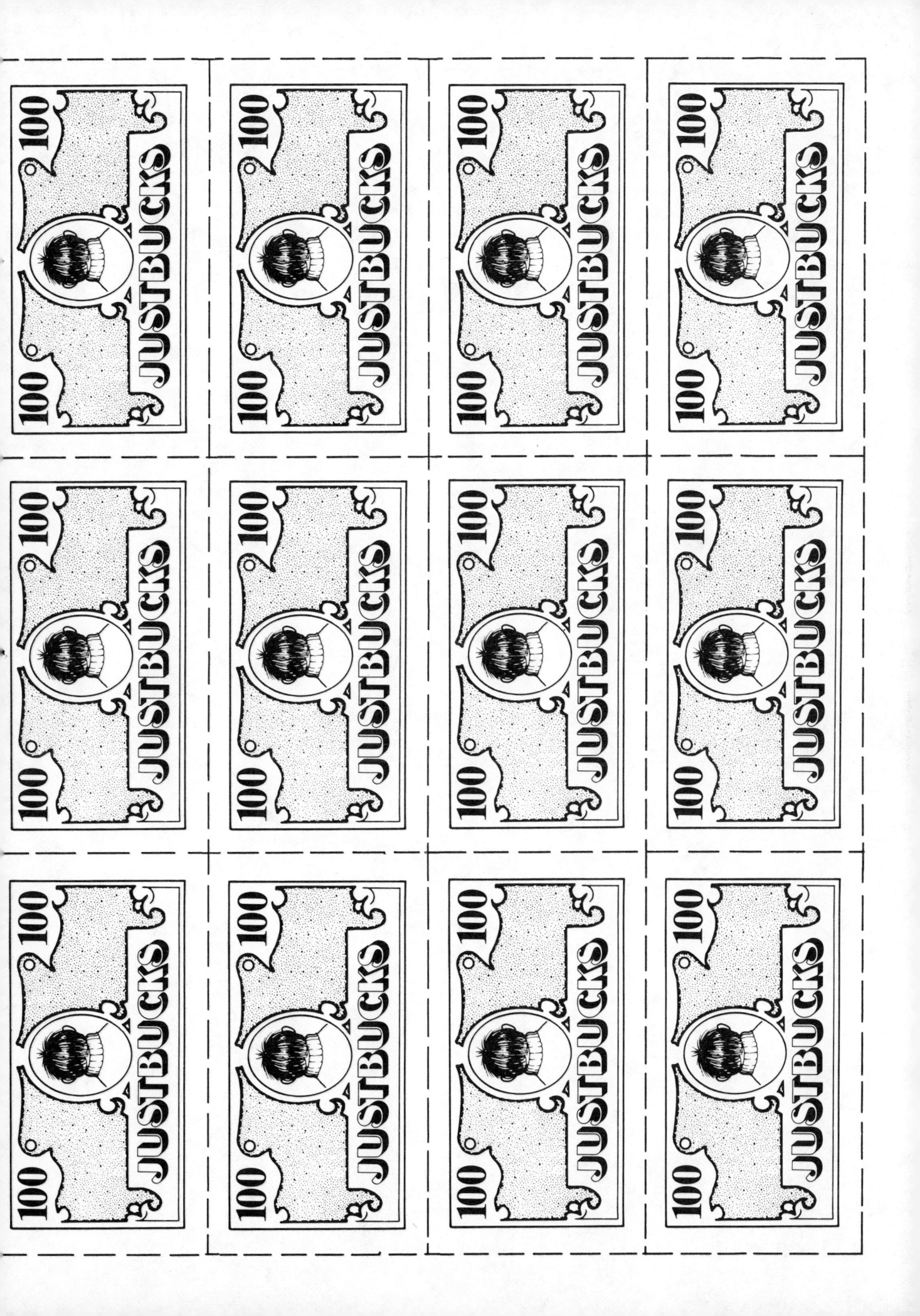

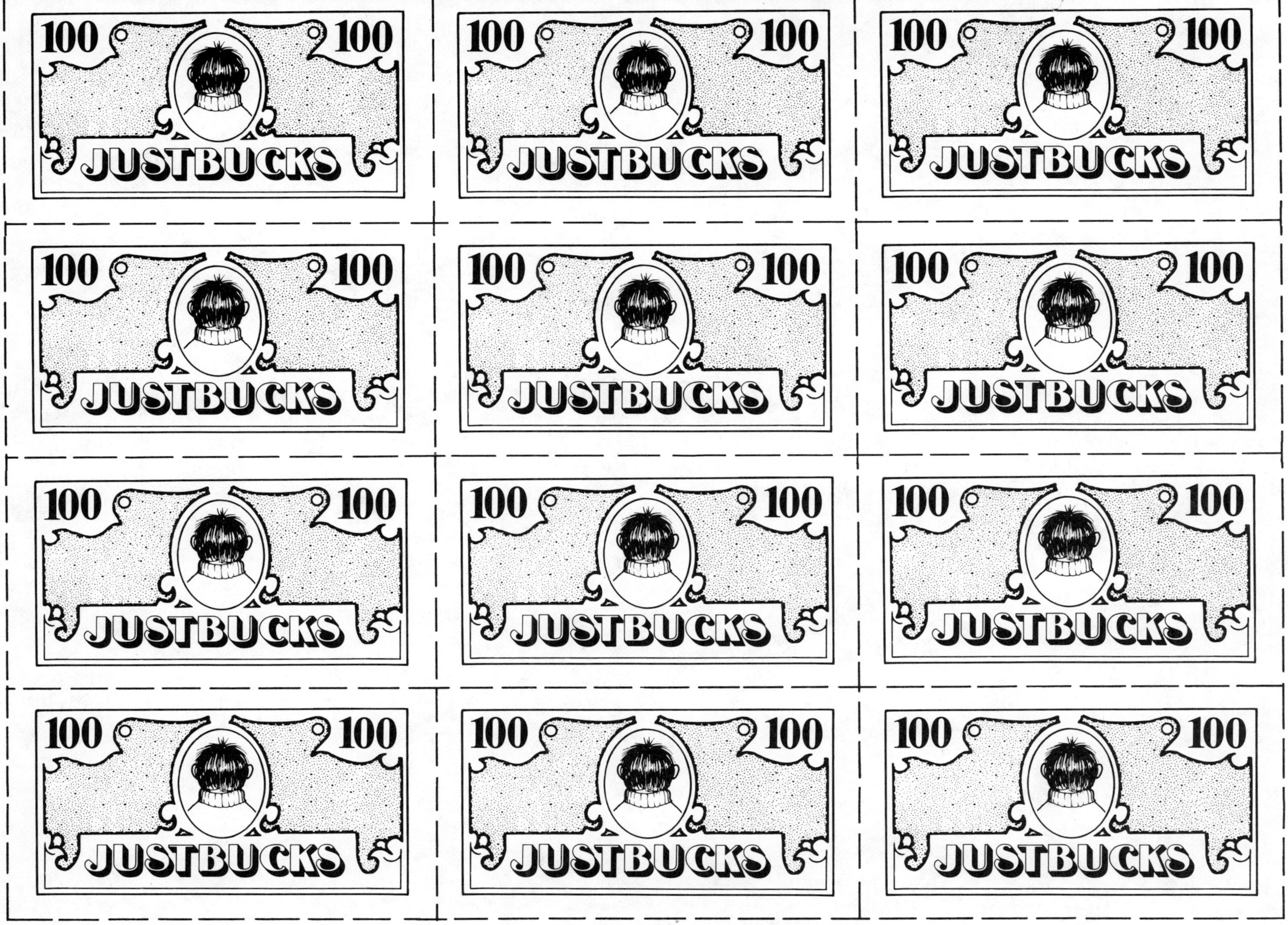
100
100
JUSTBUCKS

100
100
JUSTBUCKS

100
100
JUSTBUCKS

100
100
JUSTBUCKS

100
100
JUSTBUCKS

100
100
JUSTBUCKS

100
100
JUSTBUCKS

100
100
JUSTBUCKS

100
100
JUSTBUCKS

100
100
JUSTBUCKS

100
100
JUSTBUCKS

100
100
JUSTBUCKS

100
100
JUSTBUCKS

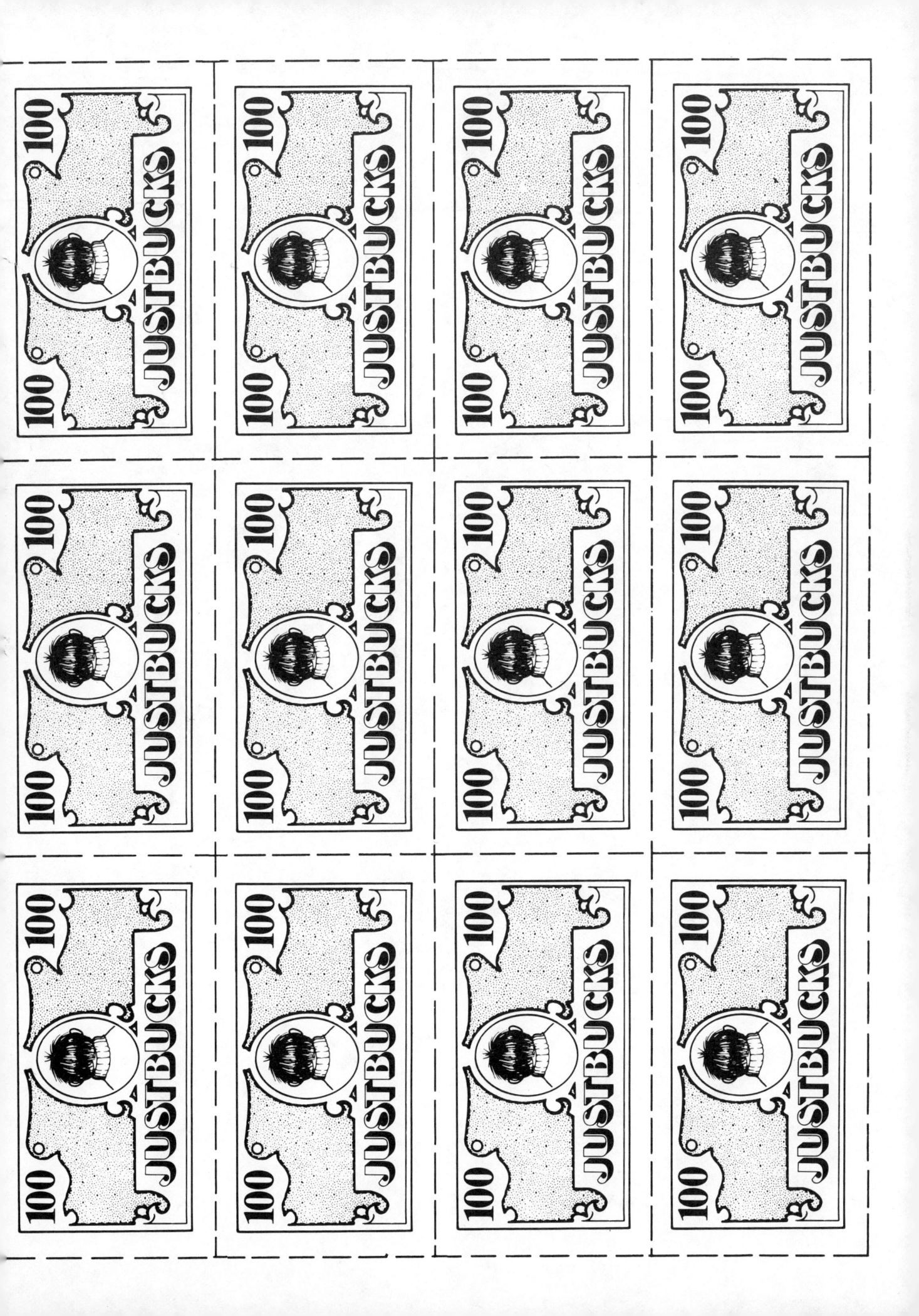

100
100
JUSTBUCKS

100
100
JUSTBUCKS

100
100
JUSTBUCKS

100
100
JUSTBUCKS

100
100
JUSTBUCKS

100
100
JUSTBUCKS

100
100
JUSTBUCKS

100
100
JUSTBUCKS

100
100
JUSTBUCKS

100
100
JUSTBUCKS

100
100
JUSTBUCKS

100
100
JUSTBUCKS

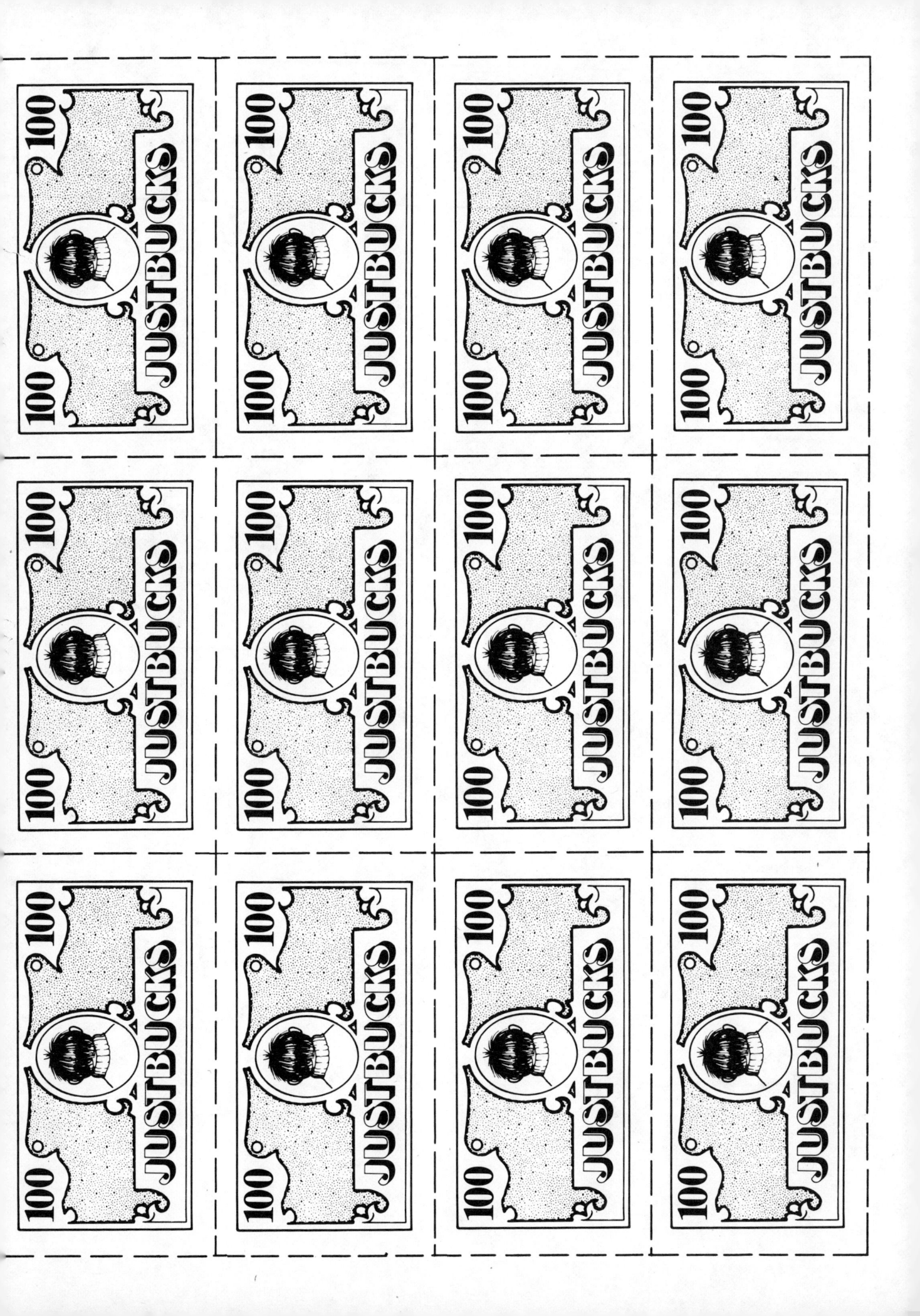

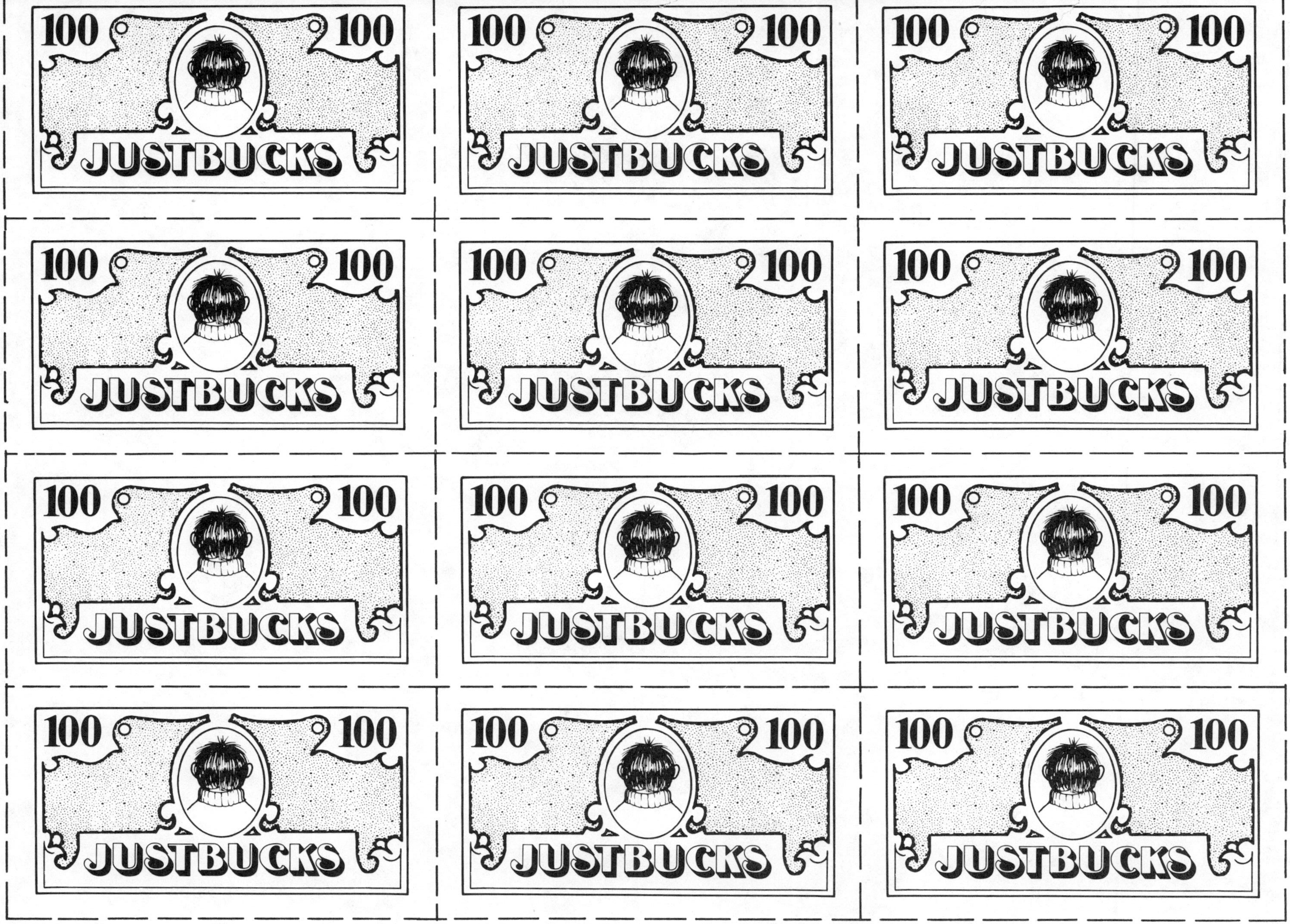
100
100
JUSTBUCKS
100
100
JUSTBUCKS
100
100
JUSTBUCKS
100
100
JUSTBUCKS
100
100
JUSTBUCKS
100
100
JUSTBUCKS
100
100
JUSTBUCKS
100
100
JUSTBUCKS
100
100
JUSTBUCKS
100
100
JUSTBUCKS
100
100
JUSTBUCKS
100
100
JUSTBUCKS

100
JUSTBUCKS
100

100
JUSTBUCKS
100

100
JUSTBUCKS
100

100
JUSTBUCKS
100

100
JUSTBUCKS
100

100
JUSTBUCKS
100

100
JUSTBUCKS
100

100
JUSTBUCKS
100

100
JUSTBUCKS
100

100
JUSTBUCKS
100

100
JUSTBUCKS
100

100
JUSTBUCKS
100

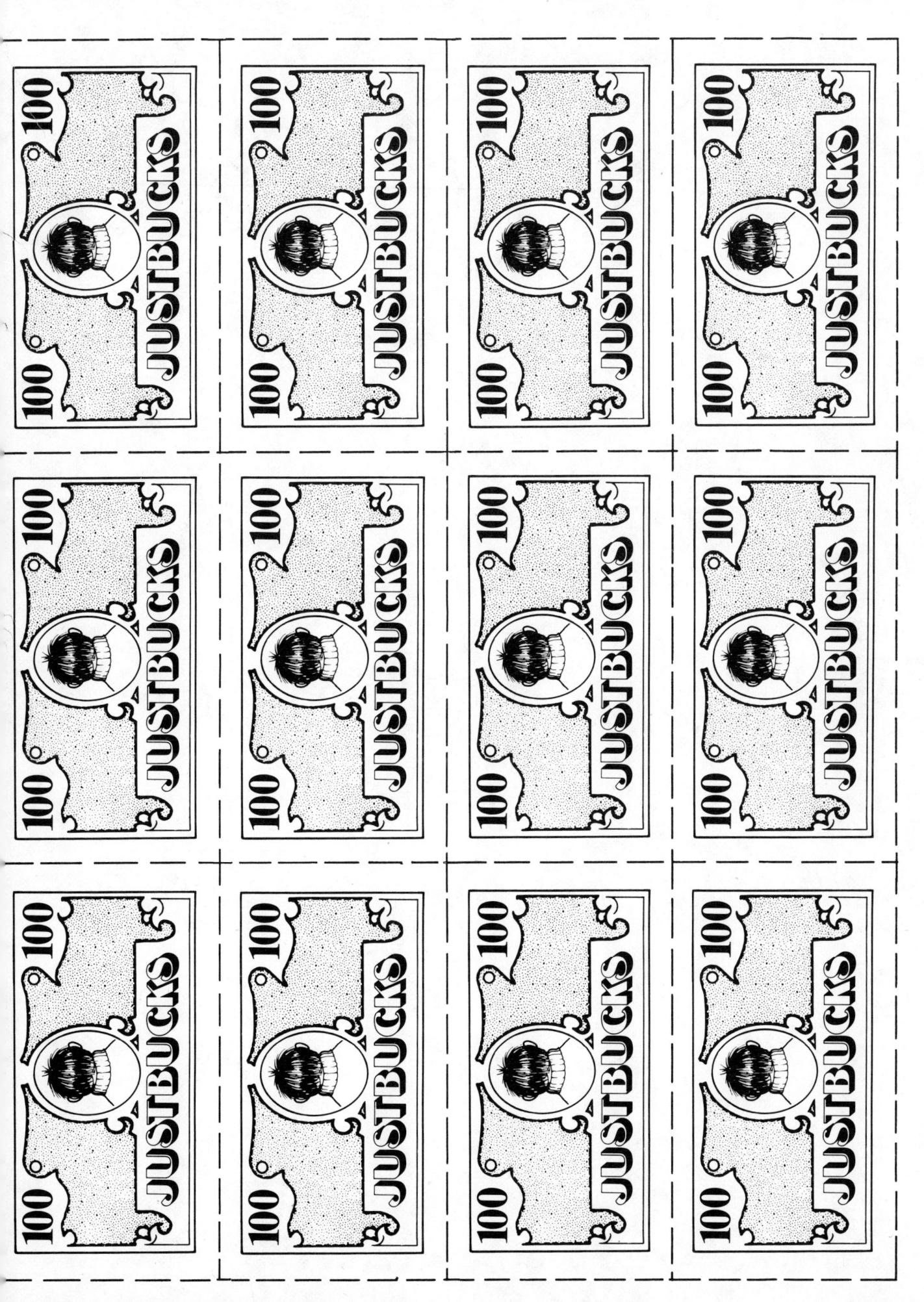